ISBN 978-1-333-98612-4
PIBN 10604115

This book is a reproduction of an important historical work. Forgotten Books uses
state-of-the-art technology to digitally reconstruct the work, preserving the original format
whilst repairing imperfections present in the aged copy. In rare cases, an imperfection in
the original, such as a blemish or missing page, may be replicated in our edition. We do,
however, repair the vast majority of imperfections successfully; any imperfections that
remain are intentionally left to preserve the state of such historical works.

For support please visit www.forgottenbooks.com

1 MONTH OF
FREE
READING

at

www.ForgottenBooks.com

By purchasing this book you are eligible for one month membership to ForgottenBooks.com, giving you unlimited access to our entire collection of over 700,000 titles via our web site and mobile apps.

To claim your free month visit: www.forgottenbooks.com/free604115

English
Français
Deutsche
Italiano
Español
Português

www.forgottenbooks.com

Mythology Photography **Fiction**
Fishing Christianity **Art** Cooking
Essays Buddhism Freemasonry
Medicine **Biology** Music **Ancient
Egypt** Evolution Carpentry Physics
Dance Geology **Mathematics** Fitness
Shakespeare **Folklore** Yoga Marketing
Confidence Immortality Biographies
Poetry **Psychology** Witchcraft
Electronics Chemistry History **Law**
Accounting **Philosophy** Anthropology
Alchemy Drama Quantum Mechanics
Atheism Sexual Health **Ancient History**
Entrepreneurship Languages Sport
Paleontology Needlework Islam
Metaphysics Investment Archaeology
Parenting Statistics Criminology
Motivational

done as much Hurt to the Christian Religion, as any Enemies secret or open, by dressing it up in such a Manner, as every Man of Understanding must despise it. This is to be seen in Popery, and others still retain many of the most odious Parts of Popery : A blind Bigotry, an implicite Faith without impartial Inquiry, and Rage against all who differ from them, with a Spirit of Persecution. But it is below Christians to render Railing for Railing, tho' it be vented in Scripture Language with great Professions of Piety. With what Sincerity or Piety our Author could hope God would bless such Endeavours so directly contrary to the Gospel, and the Method prescribed by it, upon any Offence taken, let himself account.

The

The Author's *Propositions, with Remarks on them.*

PROPOSITION I.

" W E could have the Knowledge of Moral Good
" and Evil, altho' we knew nothing of the
" Being of God. "

R E M A R K,

HE fpeaks here indefinitely, as if Mr. HUTCHESON had taught, That we could have Notions of all Sorts of Moral Good without any Knowledge of God: And then calls it blafphemous, to fay, God acts from Love of himfelf; tho' prefently we will find, in his Paper, That He did all Things for himfelf, and his own Glory.

PROP. II.

T ENDENCY to promote the Happinefs of others is the
" Standard of Moral Goodnefs. "

R E M A R K S.

TO prove this to be Mr. HUTCHESON's Tenet, you cite two Paffages from his Books, nothing to the Purpofe; and fome Paffages from the Confeffion and the Scriptures, not oppofite to this Tenet, even as you exprefs it: Only afferting, *That the Law of God is the Rule, or chief Rule of our Actions*; or, *That Sin is a Transgreffion of his Law*; which Mr. HUTCHESON never denied.

NEXT follow fine Reafons, to fhew, That the Moral Goodnefs of God is different from Benignity; otherways, his Moral Goodnefs commenced only at the Creation, and he was void of it from Eternity, even unto a Period at an infinite Diftance: I fuppofe you mean, from the Commencement of Eternity, for otherways the Creation was not at any Diftance from Eternity, or any Part of it, fince it is fuppofed to have no Parts. Now, Is not a firm, conftant Purpofe in the Divine Mind, from all Eternity, to create a World, an equal Evidence of eternal Goodnefs, as the prefent Exiftence is a Proof of prefent Goodnefs?

His

Mr. *HUTCHESON's* Propofitions.

PROPOSITION I.

WE may approve or condemn fome Sorts of Virtues and Vices, even tho' we had not known GOD, or had any Perfuafion, that, by his Laws, he required the one, and prohibited the other: We fhould, for Inftance, approve humane, friendly, grateful Actions toward our Fellows, and condemn the contrary; the very *Epicureans* did fo, who believed no Providence or Laws of God.

AGAIN, we have a Notion of Moral Goodnefs, prior, in the Order of Knowledge, to any Notion of the Will or Law of God; altho' the Moral Perfections of God are prior, in Nature, to all our Faculties.

PROP. II.

BENEVOLENT Affections toward others are our primary Notion of Moral Goodnefs, or the primary Object of our Approbation. But, as there are different Sorts of benevolent Affections, fo there are different Degrees of Moral Goodnefs: We count God morally Good, on this Account, that we juftly conclude, he has effential Difpofitions to communicate Happinefs and Perfection to his Creatures with moft perfect Wifdom, and raifed above all mean Views, oppofite to it: That we muft have another Notion of moral Goodnefs, prior to any Relation to Law, or Will, or even to effential Rectitude, or Conformity to Divine Perfection: Otherways, when we fay, *God's Laws are good*, we make no valuable Encomium on them; and only fay, God's Laws are conformable to his Laws, or, his Will is conformable to his Will. He would not then command Actions, becaufe they are good; or, prohibite them, becaufe they are evil. So, when we fay *God is morally good*, or, *excellent*, we would only mean, he is conformable to himfelt; which would be no Praife, unlefs he were previoufly known to be good.

Mr.

His Notion of Moral Goodnefs is *Poffeffion of Bleffednefs and Perfection.* Is *Bleffednefs* Happinefs of any Kind, or is it only Happinefs of a moral Kind? Then Moral Goodnefs is defined by Moral Happinefs, (no clearer than the Thing defined) and *Perfection :* Is this any natural Perfection, fuch as *Eternity, Omniprefence, Simplicity?* the Poffeffion of thefe imports no Moral Goodnefs. 'Tis then the Poffeffion of moral Perfection or moral Goodnefs ; *i. e.* the Definition of moral Goodnefs is moral Perfection. Again the fame is defined by the fame, and nothing clearer. The *contemplating his Nature with Delight* argues no Moral Goodnefs, unlefs the Qualities contemplated be previoufly known to be good, and this Goodnefs is explain'd by loving Goodnefs.

P R O P.   III.

" SElfmurder is in fome Cafes lawful.

R M A R K S.

THE Impertinence of the Scripture Proofs here is amazing ; as if Mr. Hutcheson had taught that Men might kill themfelves when they pleafed, under any Evil, even while they had further Profpects of doing good in Life, and exprefs Commands of God to endure thefe Afflictions, with Promifes of his Support, and the Affiftance of his Spirit. Whereas Mr. Hutcheson ever taught that in thefe Cafes all Suicide was unlawful. When he mentioned the Excufes, alledged by fome for the Heathens, as They had no other Guide but the Light of Nature, and were left to judge by the Probabilities they had, without any fpecial Promifes of Support, or revealed Commands to endure thefe Afflictions ; he only did, as in other controverted Cafes, candidly reprefent what is faid on both Sides. But we affert, He never approved of any, even, the moft celebrated Inftances of Suicide among them, which Chriftians have fince looked on as the moft excufable : For Example, he condemned thofe of *Lucretia, Cato,* and *Brutus.* He fhewed, that *Atticus* would have acted a far more virtuous and glorious Part, by continuing in Life, and giving an Example to all about him of Fortitude, ' Patience, and Refignation to the Divine Will ; and, as he did not, was fo far deficient in Virtue.

As for the imaginary Cafe mentioned by this Author, in which, he fays, Mr. Hutcheson thinks Suicide highly
laudable

:'MR. HUTCHESON ever maintains, That the Obfervation of the Divine Laws tends to the greateft Good of Mankind; tho' 'tis difingenoufly alledged, that he fpeaks only of Tendeney to external Good. He ever fpeaks of it as an impoffible Suppofition, contradictory in Terms, That any Sin or Violation of God's Law can tend to the abfolute Good of Mankind; tho' he teaches, with all Moralifts antient and modern, That many of the ordinary Precepts admit of Exceptions, in Cafes of fingular Neceffity.

THE Author's Reprefentations of this Doctrine fhew, either grofs Difingenuity, or Ignorance. None ever taught, Neceffity made Sin, or the breaking of God's Laws lawful.

PROP. III.

AS Mr. HUTCHESON's Doctrine on this Point is fufficiently plain, from what we have faid in the Animadverfions on this Propofition in the Author; we have only to obferve, here, that Mr. HUTCHESON's grand Aim, in his Explications of the *5th* Chapter of *Puffendorf*, where this Queftion occurs, was to infpire into his Scholars a noble Contempt of Danger, and a generous Readinefs to expofe our Lives, were it to the moft certain Death, whenever the Caufe of our Country, or the Good of Mankind requir'd it.

. HE told us, at great length, the plaufible Arguments of a great Number of Writers, in Defence of the Doctrine and Practice of many Ancients: And the Arguments on the other Side, in the moft plaufible Cafes. But we never heard him decide, as our Author alledges.

laudable; he has grofly confounded and mifreprefented it with his ufual Calumny and Abfurdity. Mr. HUTCHESON is fo far from the Opinion he is here charged with, That he reprefented the Want of Refolution to ftand all Tortures for fo noble a Caufe, as a Weaknefs of Mind, and a Want of a fufficient Force of Virtue. He always fpoke of thofe, who had rather chofen to undergo the fevereft Torments in fuch a Cafe, as Heroes worthy of the higheft Admiration, and Applaufe.

NEVER did any Man of Gravity fay *Selfmurder* was lawful in any Cafe. But our Author knew this was an odious Word, always importing Guilt. He taught it lawful to kill Men in a juft War. Our Author might as juftly have charged him with teaching the Lawfulnefs of *Murther*. But he knew the Word *Selfmurther* was fit to raife a *Popular Odium and Clamour*.

PROP. IV.

" 'TIs fometimes lawful to make a Lie.

REMARKS.

MR. HUTCHESON never fpoke fuch Words, or any e-quivalent to them. *Lying* is a Word always importing a Crime. He might as juftly have charged him with teaching Murder and Theft. The Scriptures are as wifely cited, as if One heaped together all the Texts againft Murder and Theft, and all the folemn Commands to the *Hebrews*, in *Deuteronomy*, to obferve the Laws of God ; and thence concluded that all our Divines, Moralifts and Criticks, were guilty of grofs Herefy and Deifm, for faying, " That a Man perifhing " by Hunger, when he could not, by any Intreaty or Offers " of Service, get Food to preferve Life by Confent of One " who had fuperfluous Stores, might juftly take fecretly, or " by Force, what might preferve Life : " and " that in an " overloaded Boat, 'tis lawful to caft Lots who fhould be " thrown over : " and " that it was lawful in *David* to take " the fhew Bread. "

OUR Author is fuch a deep Moralift and Cafuift, that he ventures like an Hero to encounter the whole World in deny-ing that the *Fraud* or *unjuft Violence of the Party is a juft Exception againft a Contract, efpecially if confirmed by Oath.* " He main-" tains the Validity and Obligation of the Contract obtained
" thro'

P R O P. IV.

MR. HUTCHESON ever taught, That the Law of Veracity was as facred a Precept of the Law of Nature, as, *Thou fhalt not kill: Thou fhalt not fteal*. Tho' he has alfo told us, Almoft all Writers on Morals plead, that all thefe Laws are underftood to admit Exceptions, in Cafes of great Extremity ; but ftill without deciding this Debate.

NOTHING can be a more malicious Calumny, than the Afperfion on Mr. HUTCHESON in this Place. Whoever underftands any Thing of the Bufinefs of a Profeffor of Moral Philofophy, muft know, he is obliged, in all controverted Points, to reprefent what is faid on both Sides, in a fair and juft Light. The Author could not but know this ; and was guilty of bafe Difingenuity, to reprefent, as a Man's own Opinion, what he delivered in that Manner. We affert, He never taught, as his own Sentiments, any of the Arguments he mentioned on this Head, for fubmitting Veracity to the Public Good in Cafes of urgent Neceffity : But, on the Contrary, confuted, at great length, the loofe Tenets of *Barbyrac*, as well as *Puffendorf*, in Oppofition to what he is here charged with. He dwelt long, and warmly on the high Importance of inculcating, in the ftrongeft Manner, into the Minds of Youth, an univerfal Regard to *Veracity* and *Sincerity*, in all Cafes. He conftantly taught, That the Heart has the fame ultimate Feeling of the native Beauty and Lovelinefs of Veracity and Sincerity, as of any of the other Virtues.

MR. HUTCHESON teaches, with all Moralifts and Civilians, That the Fraud or unjuft Force of one Party in a Contract, makes void the Obligation of the other, even tho' it had been confirmed by an Oath given during the Error occafioned by the Fraud, or during the Terror occafioned by

the

" thro' Fraud by the *Gibeonites*, becaufe confirmed by Oath, "
tho' the Matter of it was contrary to an exprefs Command of
God, to cut off that People. Oaths are, it feems, eafy En-
gines of eluding God's Laws; when we pleafe ; eafier than
Mr. HUTCHESON's Cafes of great Neceffity. He proves this
firft by the Judgment of the Princes of *Ifrael*, the very Judgment
in Queftion, whether juft or not ;   and then by a Proof which
no Man of common Senfe could ufe ; the Punifhment inflicted
on *Saul*'s Sons, for their Father's Breach of this Covenant :
whence he proves it obligatory. Did not our deep Author
know, that all Writers fay, it became obligatory by the fub-
fequent Ratification, after the Fraud was known to the *Ifrael-
ites*, and not in Virtue of what was obtained by Fraud ? The
Difficulty however is not at all removed, as he might fee, if
he looked into any good Writer on this Cafe. He has Learn
ing enough to affert ftrongly againft his Adverfary, which is
enough for a Man of Zeal.

PROP. V.

" 'TIs ridiculous to fpeak of the Sinfulnefs of Cards and
" Dice, or any fuch Diverfion in which Lottery
" is practifed.

R E M A R K.

H E proves this to be falfe, becaufe we find Lots folemnly
ufed in Scripture on a grand Occafion. So was Bread and
Wine, and he fhould thence infer it to be unlawful to ufe them
on any other Occafion.

PROP. VI.

" 'TIs wrong to fay, Cod always acts for his own Glory,
" or that we ought to have that End always in view.

R E M A R K S.

HE hath fubjoined here Heaps of Texts, without any
Explication of their Meaning ; Whether God's fole and
ultimate End in all his Actions, is promoting his *effential*
Glory, or his *declarative?* or, Whether we fhould, in each
Action, aim at promoting the Effential, or the Declarative ?
Whether

the unjuft Force: But limited this to fuch avowed unjuft Force as is ufed by Pyrates and Robbers, fo as not to extend to the Force ufed in Publick Solemn Wars, upon fpecious Allegations of Right. He told, what feemed to him the O- pinion not only of *Cicero*, but of *Puffendorf* and *Barbeyrac*, That, as Pyrates, Robbers, and manifeft Tyrants had renounced a Social Life, and all the Laws of Nature, we were free from all Bonds toward them in the Ufe of Speech ; and might ufe Forms of Swearing, without Intention of performing. This laft Article he directly oppofed, every Time he menti- oned it ; and ufed this very Expreffion, *That to die, rather than ufe the Name of God with Intention to violate the Oath, would be as much Martyrdom, as dying rather than renounce Chriftianity*. The Author's Charge here is directly falfe Calumny ; and yet, on this Occafion too, he can cite the Holy Scriptures.

P R O P. V.

MR. HUTCHESON faid Words to this Effect often, par- ticularly in his warm Exhortations to his Scholars to abftain from any Diverfions which might too much wafte their Time by their being agreeable : And when he was fhewing the Sin of hazarding our Fortunes, without an important Caufe, or of being covetous to obtain the Wealth of others by Gaming. Let the World judge of the Wifdom of the Charge here brought.

P R O P. VI.

MR. HUTCHESON never taught thefe Words. But at great Length fhewed the Ambiguity of the Expreffion, and explain'd in what Senfe God might be faid to act for his own Glory, and in what Senfe Men fhould act for it.

HE never arrogated to himfelf fome Criticifms the Author refers to. If he had had as much Inclination to reading, as he had to vent his good Nature in Print, he might have found thefe Criticifms in known approved Authors. This was a fine Topick however for a popular Clamour.

P R O P.

Whether promoting the Declarative means any Thing elfe, than making the Perfections of God known to Men? which muft flow from Gratitude and Love to God, and Goodwill to them, and natively tend to their Increafe in Virtue and Perfection.

P R O P.   VII.

THERE is a Superiority of Moral Good in the World.

R E M A R K S.

THE following Reafoning of the Author leads the Reader to conceive, that Mr. HUTCHESON faid there was a Superiority of Moral Good among the Adult of Mankind in this Earth.

A wicked Man is capable of doing good Actions.   This is faid here indefinitely, without any of the ufual Diftinctions of *Material* and *Formal, Natural* and *Spiritual.*   And then Heaps of Citations from the Confeffion and Scriptures about fpiritual Good, and about the Actions of profligate Perfons.

The Number of the Saved is greater than that of the Damned, becaufe all who die in Infancy are faved: And then by an Heap of Scriptures, fome of them very impertinently ufed, he infinuates as if Mr. HUTCHESON denied original Sin

The Light of Nature fufficient to Salvation.   This confuted too by many Texts of Scripture, proving that no Man can obferve the whole Law fully, and that all Salvation muft be thro' Chrift: None of thofe Points did ever Mr. HUTCHESON deny.

P R O P.   VIII.

" IT is not probable that the fame Bodies that are laid in the " Grave, fhall be raifed again at the Refurrection.

R E M A R K.

THEN are fubjoined fuch Reafoning and Texts, as if Mr. HUTCHESON had denied that any of that Matter laid in the Grave, fhould be raifed again :   And this with great Oftentations of Wifdom and Piety.

P R O P.   VII.

MR. HUTCHESON taught that in the whole of a good God's Works, or the Univerfe in all its Duration, there mnft be a great Superiority of Good : He never confined this Affertion to the Adult of Mankind.

He maintained, as every Moralift in teaching the Law of Nature muft, that many Actions of Heathens were morally good.

In anfwering *Bayle*'s Manichean Objections againft the Goodnefs of God, from the vaft Superiority of the Number of the Damned to that of the Saved, he denied that any could prove the Fact to be fo, and that from a probable Judgment that all the Children of the Heathens are not damned. This is called prying into the Counfels of God, but to damn them all, is modeft Humility, and no Prying at all, it feems.

He never faid there was any Salvation to any of fallen Mankind, except by the Merits of Chrift, but often faid, he faw no Proof, that none could reap the Benefit of his Merits, but thofe who actually knew him ; Nor do we fee it yet, either from the Scriptures cited by this Author, or the Confeffion.

P R O P.   VIII.

MR. HUTCHESON teaches, That the fame Body fhall rife again ; but, to *Samenefs of Body*, he does not make it neceffary, that all the fame Particles fhould be raifed, without any Addition or Deduction ; otherways our Bodies would not be *the fame* from Morning to Night. One muft have been very keen to find Herefy, who looked for it here. The Author fays as much himfelf on this Head.

PROP. IX.

" THE Divine Right of Dominion over the Creatures is " not properly founded upon Creation, nor upon " abfolute Dependence, nor upon Benefits received.

REMARKS.

HERE follow Heaps of Scriptures, as if Mr. HUT-CHESON had faid, that from Creation, or Benefits conferr'd, we were under no Obligations of Duty or Gratitude, or had no Motives to Obedience; which is a bafe Mifreprefentation.

AND then becaufe he argued upon the bare Suppofition of two oppofite Principles, there follows a filly Confutation of the Suppofition, as if Mr. HUTCHESON had believed it fact, or thought it a poffible or probable Scheme.

PROP. X.

" SIN is not aggravated by the infinite Majefty of God a " gainft whom it is committed. " And " 'tis a dif-" putable Point, whether the Punifhments of the Wicked are " eternal. No Man can be faid properly to fin againft God. " And the Author heartily wifhes thefe Opinions were true, if his Bible would let him, and then fuch Heaps of Texts and Reafonings as on former Articles.

PROP. IX.

MR. Hutcheson taught, That, from the Moral Per_
fections of God, we could deduce his Right of Go-
verning his Creatures, in the moſt proper Manner: Tho', at
the ſame Time, he ever ſubjoined, that Creation and Benefits were ſtrong Motives to Gratitude and Love; and, that
this Queſtion was only a ſpeculative Nicety, ſince all that ever
was alledged, as a Foundation of Dominion, by any one,
was found in the only True God. This Tenet is taught by
many zealous Calviniſts, in their Syſtems. It muſt therefore
be an highei, or a very different Sort of Zeal, which could
find Hereſy in it.

PROP. X

THE Charge againſt Mr. Hutcheson is here directly
falſe and calumnious, in theſe three Points and ſome
more, in this Article. He argüed directly, That Crimes, or
Sins, are aggravated by the Dignity of the Object againſt
whom they are committed: He taught this in Print. He ex-
preſly taught too, That however the Platoniſts, and *Ori-
gen* and ſome others, to vindicate the Goodneſs of God, ſeemed
to look for an univerſal Reſtoration of all; yet the expreſs
Words of Scripture would allow no Chriſtian to make that
Defence. He offered ſeveral Reaſons in Defence of Eternal
Puniſhments.

He ever ſaid, That Men could ſin againſt God, as well as
Men; tho' they could not hurt him. Indeed he often ſaid,
He knew not how any actual Quality of a finite Being
could be called infinite; that Hatred of God muſt be the
higheſt Guilt poſſible; but, to call all Sin infinitely evil,
when the Guilt of one Sin may ſurpaſs another ſo exceedingly,
muſt be a very diſputable Expreſſion, as it ſuppoſes one Infinite
much greater than another, in the very Reſpect in which the
other is infinite.

PROP. XI.

" THE Government of the Church belongs to the Civil
" Magiftrate. " Here he fubjoins, as if Mr.
HUTCHESON afferted, that all the Powers in the Church of
Preaching, Adminiftrating the Sacraments, Rebuking, Cen-
furing, were derived from the Magiftrate, with grofs Difingenuity: So he charges him with teaching, *That all Herefies in
Opinion, fhould pafs without any Cenfure.* That *Subfcribing a Confeffion fhould be banifhed out of the Church.* To this are fubjoined, in
Mr. HUTCHESON's Name, fome Reafonings the Author has
made for him, that he might have an Opportunity for the
good-natured Charge of Perjury on him, and many Minifters
of the Church, who, he fays, are preaching againft the Confeffion.

WE muft alfo obferve what follows upon thefe Propofiti-
ons, A Charge of perverting Texts of Scripture, in
which the Author both fhews his Malice and Ignorance. Any
Man who will look into *Pool's* Synopfis, a Book to which any
Scholar can have Accefs, will find that, *Prov.* xvi. 4. is in-
terpreted by many great Men, as Mr. HUTCHESON does. *God
fitted each Thing for itfelf, or its own Bufinefs*; Our Author has
made indeed a new Interpretation of his own in Mr. HUTCHE-
SON's Name, different from all thofe in the Criticks. So *Rom.*
xii. 11. That Reading is known to all Men of Letters to be
common in the Greek Manufcripts, and was followed by many
Fathers, as well as feveral modern Criticks, among the *Calvin-
ifts* too; and yet this Author ignorantly or malicioufly afcribes
this to Mr. HUTCHESON as a Perverfion, who told us of it
without efpoufing it.

MR. HUTCHESON faid that the Rule ufed by fome, as
a great leading Maxim, *We muft not do evil, that good may come
of it,* was not taught by the Apoftles as a Rule, nor could
be of any Service to decide any debated Point in Morals. For
often for a good End, we may do what would have been cri-
minal without a View to fuch an End, as in Amputations, hazarding

PROP. XI

MR. HUTCHESON maintains, that there are Powers of a religious Kind belonging to every Minifter, and even fome to every Chriftian, not derived from the Magiftrate : But that it belongs to the Magiftrate to take Care of the religious Notions of the People, to appoint proper Teachers, and to fupport them. This Scheme he feemed to approve moft, when mentioning two other different ones, One of the Papifts, the Other of Independents ; we cannot directly charge him with it, let it be good or bad. He alfo pleaded for univerfal Toleration by the State, toward all peaceable Subjects of whatever Religion, Let the Church cenfure their Opinions as it pleafes : And fhewed how this is reconcileable with the Magiftrate's Care of Religion.

---

zarding Life in War, delivering Money to a Robber to fave our Lives, or putting Men to Death for Defence of our Country. In other Cafes there are fome Evils we fhould not do, even to obtain thefe Ends, fuch as Blafphemy, Perjury, Abjuring the Faith. Now this Rule does not tell us what we are to do for a good End, and what not.

MR. HUTCHESON never faid that the Rule, 1 *Cor.* x. 31. was to be reftricted only to the Cafe of Eating or not eating Meats offered to Idols, or prohibited among the Jews. So all his fine Triumphs are loft.

As our Author takes upon him to direct and admonifh others, we fhall only fuggeft to him and all our Fellow-ftudents, to examine Matters well, before they charge Men in Print with Herefies, to confult Men of more Wifdom, Learning and Experience than themfelves, and to follow the charitable Precepts of the Gofpel. If he was inftigated or patronized by Men of any Character or Station, let them confider what a fine Example is fet. Other Students may fall a writing and printing againft themfelves or their Favourites, in Church or in Colleges , and how can they complain, if others follow the Example fet before them. What the Effects of fuch Paper-war may be, 'tis eafy to forefee. Mr. HUT-

CPSIA information can be obtained
at www.ICGtesting.com
Printed in the USA
BVOW07s1152050917
494010BV00015B/104/P